Habitats Big and Small

Where Animals Call Home

By Marla Tomlinson

Discover Plants and Animals
Vowel Teams
(ai, ay)

Scan this code to access the Teacher's Notes for this series or visit
www.norwoodhousepress.com/decodables

NORWOOD HOUSE PRESS

DEAR CAREGIVER, *The Decodables* series contains books following a systematic, cumulati‌ phonics scope and sequence aligned with the science of reading. Each book allows its reader to app‌ their phonics knowledge in engaging and relatable texts. The words within each text have been carefu‌ selected to ensure that readers can rely on their decoding skills as they encounter new or unfamil‌ words. They also include high frequency words appropriate for the target skill level of the reader.

When reading these books with your child, encourage them to sound out words that are unfamiliar attending to the target letter(s) and sounds. If the unknown word is an irregularly spelled high frequen‌ word or a word containing a pattern that has yet to be taught (challenge words) you may encourage yo‌ child to attend to the known parts of the word and provide the pronunciation of the unknown part(‌ Rereading the texts multiple times will allow your child the opportunity to build their reading fluency‌ skill necessary for proficient comprehension.

You can be confident you are providing your child with opportunities to build their decoding abiliti‌ which will encourage their independence as they become lifelong readers.

Happy Reading!

Emily Nudds, M.S. Ed Literacy
Literacy Consultant

Norwood House Press • www.norwoodhousepress.com
The Decodables ©2024 by Norwood House Press. All Rights Reserved.
Printed in the United States of America.
367N–082023

Library of Congress Cataloging-in-Publication Data has been filed and is available at
https://lccn.loc.gov/2023010399

Literacy Consultant: Emily Nudds, M.S.Ed Literacy
Editorial and Production Development and Management: Focus Strategic Communications In‌
Editors: Christine Gaba, Christi Davis-Martell
Photo Credits: Shutterstock: Adwo (p. 16), Aleksandra Wilert (p. 18), Anne Coatesy (p. 11),
BluesPumpkin (p. 5), Ja Crispy (p. 7), Macrovector (covers), Natasa Ivancev (p. 4), OlgaKok (p. 1‌
photostar72 (p. 19), Pina Suthaphan (p. 9), Prisma Nova Photography (p. 18), Rejean Aline
Bedard (p. 15), RobertHD (p. 19), RYosha (cover, p. 8), Slatan (p. 14), sumikophoto (p. 12), Tha‌
kaewkanya (p. 13), Tomasz Klejdysz (p. 10), valda butterworth (p. 6), Vladimir Turkenich (p. 21‌
Wes Yan Photography (p. 20), Yuliya_vector (p. 17), Zuzha (p. 6).

Hardcover ISBN: 978-1-68450-689-7   Paperback ISBN: 978-1-68404-901-1
eBook ISBN: 978-1-68404-956-1

Contents

What's in a Home?

Have you ever seen a snail in your yard or at the park? It may have been climbing up a pail or bucket. Or maybe it was near a drain or in the garden.

You may find a snail in wet places.

A land snail enjoys a rock after the rain.

his is because land snails like damp places.
heir **habitat** is in wet places in soil and leaves,
r under logs and rocks.

A habitat is where living things make their homes. It has the right things to help that animal live. Because a snail needs to keep damp, their habitat is not in a dry place. If a snail stays in a hot, dry place for too long, it isn't safe. But land snails do not live in water. They need air.

This snail lives in a damp land habitat.

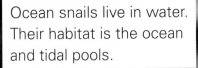

Ocean snails live in water. Their habitat is the ocean and tidal pools.

The best habitat for a land snail is near water or a place that gets rain and stays damp. A great habitat is safe and has food nearby. This keeps them alive.

A slug may look like a snail without a shell, but it is not. Both live in wet habitats. Slugs are slimy and leave a trail as they move.

These slugs are on a wet log.

Soggy Homes

Many animals need homes to keep them wet, just like the snail. Frogs live in water areas such as a swamp. They will not stray far from wet places.

There are lots of bugs for frogs to eat near water. They need fresh water to keep wet. This helps them breathe. If they fail to keep wet, they will strain to breathe and may die.

This green frog will wait for its meal to fly by.

This hippo may stay in the water for 16 hours at a time!

hippo also needs to
eep wet. The hippo spends
host of the day in water to keep its skin from getting
ry. They stay in the water when they sleep, too.
lippos will come up for air while still asleep!

lippos will also lie in mud to keep wet and
o keep safe from the sun's rays.

Homes in the Ground

Many animals make their home in the ground. Rabbits and groundhogs both make burrows for their homes. The gray mouse lives in a burrow. They may make the burrow or they may find an empty one and move in.

Mice make their homes almost anywhere! They can be found in many different types of habitats, from fields and forests to the desert! They are even found in some houses.

FUN FACT

Mice may plug the hole of their home with grass or leaves like a door to stay safe.

This mouse will wait in its home during the day and will come out at night.

The badger sett is bigger than the mouse burrow.

The badger is a **predator** of the gray mouse. Gray mice are one type of food for the badger. Badgers also eat things like worms and other bugs.

Badgers live in burrows. Their burrow home has rooms called setts. They braid tunnels to connect them. Badgers have long nails to help them dig out their home.

Like the mouse, the badger also sleeps during the day.

Busy Homes

When someone says, 'busy bee' or 'busy beaver,' they are not only saying it because it sounds fun. These animals work hard to make their homes.

A honeybee lives in a hive. They make their hives in warm, dry places near plants that have flowers. If it gets too cold, honeybees will fall asleep.

This bee may visit many flowers a day.

Bees are busy visiting flowers all day long. They bring the **nectar** back to the hive to make honey. Their habitats are in fields or orchards so they can do this job.

Some bees build their hive in a tree to keep safe from rain and predators.

A beekeeper is someone who makes homes for the bees. They take care of them and keep them safe. The keeper builds the hives in a field or near flowering plants to make the home a place the bees would want to stay.

Beekeepers make the bee habitat in a way that will keep the bees safe. These habitats are boxes with trays where the bees make their hives.

Beekeepers may have many hives in a row.

The keeper will take out the tray to get to the honey.

This beaver swims with mud to make its dam.

Beavers also spend a lot of time making their homes. They live in a lodge and build dams to keep safe. Beavers have a long, flat tail and webbed feet that help them sail through the water.

A dam is made from sticks, logs, mud, and **clay**. The beaver makes a dam to keep its habitat safer. The dam traps water. It drains slowly or not at all. This makes a pond or lake that the beaver can then build its home in.

15

Beavers use their teeth to saw down a tree. It sounds like a pain, but their teeth are big and made to bite through wood. They bring that wood to where they are building their home.

After a few trees and sticks are laid, the beaver will pat mud or clay over it to keep it in place.

A dam makes water drain very slowly to make a safe pond for the beavers.

Big Homes

Ants build a home that can go deep underground. They dig out the sand and dirt, grain by grain. Their home is called a colony. From the outside it looks plain. An ant hill is small. But inside it has many rooms and layers. It can hold many active ants. Some colonies hold over 1,000 ants!

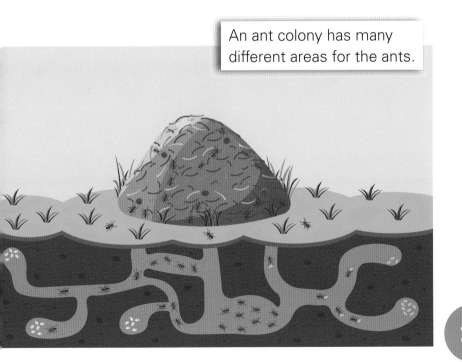

An ant colony has many different areas for the ants.

The **sociable** weaver is an African bird that makes a home that has many rooms. The nest is made with hay. These nests are some of the biggest of any bird. They can hold over 100 birds. The chain of nests is built together to be home to many families, like an apartment building. This bird feeds on bugs and seeds.

FUN FACT

Sociable weavers take care of younger siblings and other hatchlings.

The sociable weaver nest may take up most of a tree.

These friendly weavers look out from one of the holes in their nest.

Homes Made By People

There are many animals that live in homes made by people. One main place where animals live with people on farms.

Cows and horses live on farms. They feed on hay, grass, and oats.

Quail live on farms. Farmers raise them just like chickens. People pay for their eggs.

This horse is eating some hay.

This quail rests on some hay.

19

Chickens can make their home in a coop on a farm. They eat seeds and grain. Coops are safe spaces for hens to lay eggs.

Chickens can fly, but not very far. They are not good at it. It may look like they just **flail** around.

Chickens are not very good at flying.

Safe at Home

An animal home needs to **protect** the animal and its babies.

The kind of home changes based on what the animal needs. Does it like heat or to be cool? Wet or dry? The animal may need to hide in its home or be able to **flee**.

If the home is right, the animal will be happy and may not stray too far!

This raccoon has made its home in this tree.

Glossary

clay: damp earth that can be used to make bricks or pots

flail: move fast and wild

flee: rush away

habitat: the natural place where an animal or plant can live and grow

nectar (nēk-tər): sweet liquid found in many flowers

predator (prĕd-ə-tər): an animal that hunts other animals for food

protect (prō-tĕct): look after and keep safe

sociable (sō-shĕ-bŭl): likes being with others; very friendly

Index

Vowel Teams

ai				ay		
braid	laid	plain	snail	clay	lay	stray
chain	main	quail	strain	day	may	tray
drain	nails	rain	tail	gray	pay	way
fail	pail	raise	trail	hay	stay	
flail	pain	sail	wait			
grain						

High-Frequency Words

after	around	does	great	most	says	too
air	because	even	houses	move	small	very
also	changes	found	kind	over	sounds	work
animal	different	good	live	right	through	

Challenging Words

active	climbing	colony	layers
badger	colonies	hold	type